LANDMA

Landmark Productions
presents the world premiere of

The Approach

by Mark O'Rowe

The world premiere of *The Approach* took place at
Project Arts Centre, Dublin, on 6 February 2018.

Dublin City
Baile Átha Cliath

ACKNOWLEDGEMENTS

Landmark Productions would like to thank the Abbey Theatre; Lian Bell; Sarah Baxter; Richard Cook; Jasmine Daines Pilgrem; Druid Theatre Company; Samira Higham; Julie Kelleher, Sean Kelly and all at The Everyman; Nick Marston, Camilla Young and Katie Battcock at Curtis Brown; Derick Mulvey; Conor Naughton; Trevor Price; Tom Rohan; Aoife Ruane; Declan Ryder; Jonathan Shankey; Stage Sound Services; Oddie Sherwin; Owen Sherwin; Rachel West; Eleanor White; Jonathan White; Cian O'Brien, JC Collins, Carmel Mackey, Siobhan Shortt, Melanie Wright, and all the Front-of-House, box office and technical staff of Project Arts Centre.

Cover: photography by Patrick Redmond; graphic design by Gareth Jones.

The Approach is funded through an Arts Council Theatre Project Award.

Landmark Productions
presents

The Approach
by Mark O'Rowe

CAST

in order of speaking

Cora	Cathy Belton
Anna	Aisling O'Sullivan
Denise	Derbhle Crotty

Director	Mark O'Rowe
Set and Lighting Designer	Sinead McKenna
Costume Designer	Joan O'Clery
Sound Designer	Philip Stewart

Production Manager	Eamonn Fox
Stage Director	Clive Welsh
Assistant Stage Manager	Emma Coen
Costume Supervisor	Nicola Burke
Hair and Make-Up	Val Sherlock

LX Programmer	Eoin McNinch
Set Construction	TPS
Scenic Artist	Sandra Butler
Crew	Hugh Roberts

Producer	Anne Clarke
Associate Producer	Sara Cregan
Publicist	Sinead O'Doherty | Gerry Lundberg PR
Marketing	Sinead McPhillips
Photographer	Patrick Redmond
Graphic Design	Gareth Jones

The play is set in Dublin.
Running time: 1 hour and 15 minutes without an interval.

www.theapproach.ie

LANDMARK

LANDMARK PRODUCTIONS
Producer

Landmark Productions is one of Ireland's leading theatre producers. Led by Anne Clarke, the company produces wide-ranging and ambitious work in Ireland and tours Irish work overseas.

Since its first production in 2004, the company has produced twenty-seven plays – including seven Irish premieres and fourteen world premieres – in Dublin.

Its productions include the Irish premieres of David Hare's *Skylight*, Edward Albee's *The Goat, or Who is Sylvia?*, Glen Berger's *Underneath the Lintel*, David Harrower's *Knives in Hens* and his Olivier Award-winning play *Blackbird*.

Recent work includes Enda Walsh's *The Walworth Farce*, starring Brendan Gleeson, Brian Gleeson and Domhnall Gleeson, together with the multi-award-winning musical *Once*, which recently played for a third successive year at the Olympia Theatre in Dublin.

Landmark's co-productions with Galway International Arts Festival include three plays by Enda Walsh: the world premieres of *Arlington* (Galway/Abbey Theatre Dublin/St Ann's Warehouse, New York) and *Ballyturk* (Galway/Olympia Theatre/Cork Opera House/National Theatre, London/Abbey Theatre Dublin/St Ann's Warehouse, New York); together with *Misterman*, starring Cillian Murphy, which toured to St Ann's Warehouse in New York and to the National Theatre in London.

Mark O'Rowe's *Howie the Rookie*, starring Tom Vaughan-Lawlor, played at the Barbican in London and at BAM in New York, where it was co-presented by Irish Arts Center as part of BAM's 2014 Next Wave season.

Other recent productions include the world premieres of two operas by Donnacha Dennehy and Enda Walsh, *The Last Hotel* and *The Second Violinist*, both co-produced with Wide Open Opera. *The Last Hotel* had its world premiere at the Edinburgh International Festival in 2015, before touring to the Royal Opera House in London, Dublin Theatre Festival, St Ann's Warehouse in New York and Les Théâtres de la Ville, Luxembourg. A film version of the opera, commissioned by Sky Arts under its Amplify programme and co-produced with Brink Films, was broadcast in April 2016. *The Second Violinist* had its world premiere at the 2017 Galway International Arts Festival and subsequently played at the Dublin Theatre Festival. Winner of the prestigious FEDORA-Generali Prize for Opera, it will play at the Barbican in London in September 2018.

Woyzeck in Winter, starring Patrick O'Kane and Camille O'Sullivan, had its world premiere, again in co-production with GIAF, at Galway International

Arts Festival in July 2017 and subsequently played at the Barbican in London and at the Dublin Theatre Festival.

Over the past decade, Landmark has produced four hugely successful plays featuring the character of Ross O'Carroll-Kelly, all of which starred Rory Nolan as Ross: Paul Howard's *The Last Days of the Celtic Tiger*, *Between Foxrock and a Hard Place*, *Breaking Dad* and *Postcards from the Ledge*.

Forthcoming productions include the stage adaptation of Louise O'Neill's book *Asking for It*, a co-production with The Everyman, which is co-commissioned by Ireland's national theatre, the Abbey, and will have its world premiere as part of Cork Midsummer Festival in June 2018 before playing on the main stage of the Abbey in November 2018.

Grief is the Thing with Feathers by Max Porter, adapted and directed by Enda Walsh and starring Cillian Murphy, produced by Complicité and Wayward Productions in association with Landmark Productions and Galway International Arts Festival, will have its world premiere at the Black Box Theatre, Galway, in March 2018.

Many of these productions would not have come to pass, or would not have toured so widely, without the support of the Arts Council / An Chomhairle Ealaíon and Culture Ireland, and Landmark is very grateful for that support.

Landmark Productions received the Judges' Special Award in The Irish Times Irish Theatre Awards for 2011, in recognition of its 'sustained excellence in programming and for developing imaginative partnerships to bring quality theatre to the Irish and international stage.' Anne Clarke received the Special Tribute Award in The Irish Times Irish Theatre Awards for 2015, in recognition of her work as 'a producer of world-class theatre in the independent sector in Ireland'.

Producer | Anne Clarke
Associate Producer | Sara Cregan

www.landmarkproductions.ie

MARK O'ROWE
Writer and Director

Mark O'Rowe is a writer and director.

His plays include *From Both Hips* (Fishamble Theatre Company, 1997); *Howie the Rookie* (Bush Theatre, 1999); *Made in China* (Peacock Theatre, 2001); *Crestfall* (Gate Theatre, 2003); *Terminus* (Peacock Theatre, 2007) and *Our Few and Evil Days* (Abbey Theatre, 2014).

He has also adapted several works, including *Hedda Gabler* (Abbey Theatre, 2015) and *DruidShakespeare*, an amalgamation of four of Shakespeare's history plays (Druid Theatre Company, 2015).

Screenplays include *Intermission* (2003), *Boy A* (2007), *Perrier's Bounty* (2009), and *Broken* (2012). He recently wrote and directed the film *The Delinquent Season*, which will be released in early 2018.

SINEAD MCKENNA
Set and Lighting Designer

Sinead has received two Irish Times Theatre Awards for Best Lighting Design and a Drama Desk nomination for Best Lighting Design for a Musical.

Previous designs for Landmark include *Howie the Rookie, Greener, October, The Last Days of the Celtic Tiger* and *Blackbird*.

Recent designs include *Grace Jones – Bloodlight and Bami* (Blinder Films); *Angela's Ashes The Musical, Futureproof* (Everyman, Cork); *Nivelli's War* (Cahoots NI/New Victory Theatre).

Other theatre designs include *The Master Builder, Richard III* and *Uncle Vanya* (West Yorkshire Playhouse); *The Beckett/Pinter/Friel Festival, Private Lives* (2016 and 2008), *Juno and the Paycock, A Month in the Country, The Gigli Concert, The Mariner, The Price* and *An Ideal Husband* (Gate Theatre); *Maz and Bricks* (Fishamble); *Fire Below* (The Lyric and Abbey Theatre); *What Put the Blood, The Wake, Othello, Aristocrats, Quietly, Alice in Funderland, The Plough and the Stars, 16 Possible Glimpses, The Burial at Thebes, Howie the Rookie, Finders Keepers* (Abbey Theatre); *The New Electric Ballroom* (Druid); *Dubliners* (Corn Exchange); *Famished Castle, Travesties, The Importance of Being Earnest, Improbable Frequency* (Drama Desk nomination 2009, Best Lighting Design for a Musical), *The Parker Project, Life is a Dream, Attempts on her Life* and *Dream of Autumn* (Rough Magic); *The Wolf and Peter, Agnes, Pageant, Swept* (CoisCéim); *Invitation to a Journey* (CoisCéim/Fishamble/ Crash Ensemble); *Don Giovanni* (OTC); *La Traviata* (Malmö Opera House); *The Rape of Lucretia* (IYO); *The Magic Flute, The Marriage of Figaro* (Opera Theatre Company); *A Midsummer Night's Dream* (Opera Ireland).

She has also worked with Decadent, Gare St Lazare, Corn Exchange, THISISPOPBABY, Siren, The Lyric, Second Age, Performance Corporation, Semper Fi and Gúna Nua.

JOAN O'CLERY
Costume Designer

Three-time winner of The Irish Times Irish Theatre Award for Best Costume Design, Joan has originated the costumes for several world premieres by major Irish writers, including Seamus Heaney, Brian Friel, Tom Murphy and Frank McGuinness. Her costumes are regularly seen on many stages around Ireland. Highlights of her costuming work include *Macbeth* at the RSC; *An Enemy of the People* at the Gate Theatre; *DruidMurphy*, a trilogy of Tom Murphy plays; and *She Stoops to Conquer* at the Abbey Theatre. For Landmark she has costumed *The Second Violinist* (co-produced with Wide Open Opera) and *Woyzeck in Winter* (co-produced with Galway International Arts Festival). Twice nominated for IFTA awards for her screen work, films include *King of the Travellers; Swansong; Snap; Out of Innocence;* and Mark O'Rowe's feature debut *The Delinquent Season*. Opera designs include *La Traviata* for the ENO and *Dubliners* for Wexford Festival Opera.

PHILIP STEWART
Sound Designer

Philip has written music and sound design for a broad range of media including theatre, sculptural and sound installations, dance, shorts, and documentary film-making. He studied composition under Donnacha Dennehy and Roger Doyle.

Recent theatre credits include *Crestfall* by Mark O'Rowe (Druid); *The Wake* by Tom Murphy, *Conservatory* by Michael West, *Hedda Gabler* by Henrik Ibsen, *Quietly* by Owen McCafferty (Abbey Theatre) and *Breaking Dad* by Paul Howard and *Howie the Rookie* by Mark O'Rowe (Landmark Productions).

He has been nominated for an Irish Times Theatre Award for his work on *The Early Bird* by Leo Butler (Natural Shocks) and *An Enemy of the People* by Henrik Ibsen (Gate Theatre).

CATHY BELTON
Cora

Cathy is thrilled to be working with Landmark again after playing Kyra in the company's acclaimed inaugural production of *Skylight*.

Recent theatre credits include *Aristocrats, The Hanging Gardens, The House, John Gabriel Borkman* with Alan Rickman (Abbey Theatre); *A View from the Bridge, A Woman of No Importance* (Gate Theatre); *Women in Arms* (Storytellers – Irish Times Best Supporting Actress nomination); *Wonderful Tennessee* (Sheffield Theatre) and the Irish premiere of Frank McGuinness' one-woman play *The Match Box* (Galway International Arts Festival – Irish Times Best Actress Award nomination). She recently appeared in Druid Theatre Company's production of *Helen and I*, directed by Annabelle Comyn.

Cathy's recent screen credits include *Philomena; A Little Chaos,* directed by Alan Rickman; and *My Name Is Emily,* directed by Simon Fitzmaurice.

Television credits include the new Alison Spittle TV series *Nowhere Fast* (Deadpan Productions, RTÉ); the series regular role of Patricia in *Red Rock* for TV3, produced by Element/Company Pictures; *Scúp* (Stirling Television/TG4/RTÉ); and *Roy* (Jam Media Ireland/CBBC (UK)/BBC) – BAFTA Children's Awards for Best Drama and Best Writer, and IFTA nomination for Best Supporting Actress for TV.

Cathy will soon appear as Mrs Hartright in the new BBC1 TV series *The Woman in White*.

DERBHLE CROTTY
Denise

Theatre includes *Hamlet, The Home Place* (Harold Pinter Theatre); *Afterplay, Juno and the Paycock, Dancing at Lughnasa* (Gate Theatre, Dublin); *Anna Karenina, Sive, The Dead, Marble, Tales of Ballycumber, An Ideal Husband, Three Sisters* (winner, Irish Times Theatre Awards Best Actress 2008), *A Month in the Country, The Plough and the Stars, The Well of the Saints, The Dandy Dolls, Bailegangaire, Portia Coughlan, The Mai, Katie Roche* (Abbey and Peacock Theatres); *DruidShakespeare* (winner, Irish Times Theatre Awards Best Actress 2015), *The Gigli Concert, The Good Father, Sive, The Silver Tassie* (Druid); *Hecuba, Macbeth, Macbett, I'll Be the Devil, Little Eyolf* (Royal Shakespeare Company); *The Playboy of the Western World, Summerfolk, The Merchant of Venice* (National Theatre, London); *The Alice Trilogy, Portia Coughlan, The Weir* (Royal Court); *The Events, The Beauty Queen of Leenane* (Young Vic); *The Seagull, Dubliners, Everyday*

(Corn Exchange); *The Field*, *Sive* (Gaiety Theatre); *Best Man* (Everyman, Cork); *The Winter's Tale* (Corcadorca) and *Thirteen* (ANU).

Television includes *Come Home, Paula* (BBC) and *Citizen Lane* and *The Clinic* (RTÉ).

Film includes *Noble*, *Stella Days*, *Joy*, *Notes on a Scandal*, *Inside I'm Dancing*, *The Merchant of Venice*, *Poorhouse*.

Derbhle is an associate artist of Druid Theatre Company, and of the Royal Shakespeare Company.

AISLING O'SULLIVAN
Anna

Aisling is an associate artist with Druid Theatre Company. Aisling's previous work for Druid includes Maureen in *The Beauty Queen of Leenane*, Maggie in *Big Maggie*, Hal/Henry V in *DruidShakespeare*, Dolly in *Bailegangaire*, The Colleen Rua in *The Colleen Bawn*, Widow Quinn in *The Playboy of the Western World* (Irish Times Theatre Award for Best Supporting Actress).

For the Abbey Theatre she played Vera in *The Wake*, Catherine in *Marble*, Lily in *Lay Me Down Softly*, Nuala in *The Cavalcaders*, Maeve in *Famine* and Maggie in *The Power of Darkness*.

Other theatre work includes Olive Day in *Crestfall* (Gate Theatre); Miss Julie in *Miss Julie* (Haymarket Theatre, London); The Duchess in *The Duchess of Malfi* (Royal Shakespeare Company); Solange in *The Maids* (Young Vic); Katherina in *Slavs* (Hampstead Theatre); Jessica in *Hysteria* (Royal Court); The File in *Mutabilitie*, Croce in *Liolà* and Slippy Helen in *The Cripple of Inishmaan* (National Theatre, London); and Pegeen Mike in *The Playboy of the Western World* (Almedia Theatre, London).

Film and television work includes *Dark Lies the Island*; *The Secret Scripture*; *Snap*; *The Butcher Boy*; *Raw* (series 2 to 5); *The Clinic* (series 1 to 5; Irish Film and Television Award for Best Actress); and *Cracker*.

EAMONN FOX
Production Manager

Eamonn is delighted to be working with the Landmark team again on *The Approach*.

He is a freelance Production Manager/Event Controller, plying his trade in the theatre, arts, television and entertainment world. By this stage in his career, he should have grown up, having worked for Galway International Arts Festival, Dublin Theatre Festival, St. Patrick's Festival, The Volvo Ocean Race 2009/2012, A Nation's Voice 2016 and extensively with Landmark Productions, Druid Theatre Company, MCD and Shinawil.

CLIVE WELSH
Stage Manager

Clive has previously worked with Landmark on *Howie the Rookie* (Project Arts Centre/Barbican/BAM), *Once* (Olympia), *Ballyturk*, in co-production with Galway International Arts Festival (National Theatre, London/Abbey Theatre), *The Talk of the Town* (Project Arts Centre) and *These Halcyon Days* (Edinburgh).

Recent credits include *Angela's Ashes* (Pat Moylan Productions); *A Christmas Carol* (The Ark); *Helen and I* (Druid); RTÉ *Centenary Concert* (Bord Gáis Energy Theatre) and touring extensively with CoisCéim Dance Theatre, including the Guthrie Theater Minneapolis, City Center New York, Centre Culturel Irlandais Paris, DanceBase Edinburgh, The Brighton Festival and Peak Performances New Jersey USA.

Work in opera includes *Margherita*, *Vanessa*, *Le Pré aux Clercs*, *Thérèse*, *La Navarraise*, *The Golden Ticket*, *The Ghosts of Versailles*, *Italian Postcard* (Wexford Festival Opera).

Clive also works on large-scale arena events and television.

NICOLA BURKE
Costume Supervisor

Nicola graduated from IADT Dún Laoghaire in 2013 with a degree in Costume Design. Since graduating, Nicola has designed numerous productions for both stage and screen. Her long history with Sickle Moon Productions includes two short films, *Splintered Concerto* and *Chimneys*. Theatre design credits include *The Strange Case of Dr Jekyll and Mr Hyde* and *Slippers* (Theatre Upstairs) and *Cirque des Rêves* (Boys School, Smock Alley). Other design credits include *The Fallen* (Irish Writers Centre); *Brontë* (Illustrated Productions); several event pieces with Arial Cirque; and *Cinderella* (Smock Alley Theatre). Theatre credits include Wardrobe Mistress for *Once* (Landmark Productions); costume co-ordination for *The Wolf and Peter* (CoisCéim); touring Europe with *Riverdance* as Wardrobe Assistant and Wardrobe Mistress; and costume assistant on many productions at the Gate Theatre.

THE APPROACH

Mark O'Rowe

For Aoife Ruane

Characters

CORA
ANNA
DENISE

This text went to press before the end of rehearsals and so may differ slightly from the play as performed.

ANNA *and* CORA *sit at a table.*

CORA. I love your bracelet, actually.

ANNA. This?

CORA. Yeah, can I have a look?

ANNA. Of course. (*Taking it off and giving it to her.*) I only got it, like, a week or two ago.

CORA. How much was it?

ANNA. Eighty-nine euro?

CORA. That's not bad.

ANNA. Sure it's not? I actually saw one on a woman in Marks and Spencer's and had to go over and ask where she got it.

CORA. And where did she get it?

ANNA. Weirs. You know on Grafton Street?

CORA. Uh-huh.

ANNA. So I went in, whenever, the following weekend and got myself one. You know who I met on the way there, actually?

CORA. Who? (*Handing it back.*) It's gorgeous, Anna.

ANNA. Thanks. Remember Emily Dowling?

CORA. Yeah.

ANNA. Her mother.

CORA. Oh, really. How was she?

ANNA. She was okay. Very haggard looking, actually.

CORA. Right. Well, she would be, though, wouldn't she.

ANNA. No, but remember how stunning she was back then?

CORA. And did you speak to her?

ANNA. Yeah…

CORA. I *do* remember.

ANNA.…just for a minute or two. She was asking how I was getting on in life. Was I married…

CORA. Right.

ANNA.…had I kids, whatever…

CORA. And did she talk about Emily?

ANNA. Yeah, a bit.

CORA. What was she saying?

ANNA. Just that she misses her still.

CORA. Uh-huh. And what else?

ANNA. Nothing else. Just weird to have met her, you know?

CORA. Mm.

Pause.

Emily. Jesus.

ANNA. Yeah, I know. Remember the sandals?

CORA. God. No, what *I* re…

ANNA. Horrible.

CORA. Absolutely.

ANNA. Sorry.

CORA. No, just saying, that time she ran away…

ANNA. Oh, *that* was fucked. Up the mountain?

CORA. Yeah.

ANNA. That was *weird*, now.

CORA. You know what was weird? No, it was, all right, but you know what was *freaky*?

ANNA. What?

CORA. ...Or *I* thought it was. The fact that she stayed up there so fucking *long*...

ANNA. No, I know.

CORA. ...without any heat or whatever, shelter. I mean, I wouldn't have lasted one night, let alone three.

ANNA. I wouldn't have gone up there in the first place.

CORA. Mm.

Beat.

ANNA. She had a fire, though, didn't she?

CORA. Did she? Oh, that's right.

ANNA. Sure that's how they spotted her.

CORA (*on 'her'*). That's right. But still, though, you know?

ANNA. Oh, no, definitely. (*Beat.*) Hard to comprehend.

CORA. Her doing it?

ANNA. Hm?

CORA. Her running away?

ANNA. Any of it. The running away...

CORA. Well...

ANNE. ...the suicide...

CORA. No, I know, but the problem was, though, I mean, I remember in school...

ANNA. Well, she wouldn't talk to you.

CORA. Right.

ANNA. I mean, ever. That's right. I mean, there were several times before *and* after she ran away I tried to communicate with her...

CORA. Yeah, me too.

ANNA. You were *very* good to her, actually, were you not?

CORA. Well, I tried to be, but you know what? If you want my help, then give me some *indication* you want it, you know? I remember once, a free class in the assembly hall, all right? Forty-five minutes I tried to engage with her. And nothing…

ANNA. Right.

CORA. …Blood from a fucking, I dunno…

ANNA. A stone.

CORA. Hm?

ANNA. Blood from a stone.

CORA. Well, it was. I mean, you do your best to be nice to, or to connect to someone, but after a while you just kind of have to admit to yourself, I mean, don't you…?

ANNA. No, you do.

CORA. …that you're wasting your time, you know?

ANNA. Mm.

Long pause.

CORA. Have you lost weight?

ANNA. Have I lost weight?

CORA. Yeah.

ANNA (*beat*). A little bit, maybe, why?

CORA. You look like you have. How much?

ANNA. About a half a stone.

CORA. You're joking! How?

ANNA. Just eating less…

CORA. Right.

ANNA. Eating better…

CORA. And are you exercising?

ANNA. Not too much, now, no. Giving up snacks at night, I think, was the main, you know, contribution.

CORA. Really.

ANNA. Mm.

CORA. What kind of snacks?

ANNA. Same as always.

CORA. Chocolate.

ANNA. Chocolate, cheese on toast or whatever. *You* look well as well, though.

CORA. No, I don't.

ANNA. Are *you* exercising? You do.

CORA. Not really. Well, yeah…

ANNA. You are.

CORA. …well, I walk a bit, I suppose, you know, like, taking Bridie out or whatever. Although…

ANNA (*on 'Although'*). Do you still have Bridie?!

CORA. Ah, yeah.

ANNA. Jesus, how is she?

CORA. She's fine. She's getting old, poor thing…

ANNA. Oh, no.

CORA. …so, yeah, so we only get out, like, now and again to be honest.

ANNA. Right. And how's *your* diet?

CORA. Not great.

ANNA. Really? What's *your* weakness?

CORA. Same as always. Crisps.

ANNA. Okay.

CORA. *Any*thing savoury, really. I had two packets the other night. And…

ANNA. No!

CORA. And I could've managed a third.

ANNA. That's not *every* night, though, is it?

CORA. No, but…

ANNA. Right.

CORA. …God, far from it, but I really need to cut that kind of shit out, you know?

ANNA. Well, now and again is okay.

CORA. I suppose.

ANNA (*beat*). And how's work? Are you still in Corrigan's?

CORA. Yeah, for my sins.

ANNA. 'For your sins'! It's not *that* bad, is it?

CORA. No, sure it's fine.

ANNA. And whatever happened with that one you were having trouble with?

CORA. Fiona?

ANNA. I can't remember her name.

CORA. Fiona. No, she's gone.

ANNA. She's gone?

CORA. Yeah.

ANNA. The wagon. She was jealous of you, you know that?

CORA. Yeah, I dunno.

ANNA. It's the only explanation, Cora. (*Beat*.) So, when did she leave?

CORA. Not long after I told you about her.

ANNA. When was that?

CORA. A year ago? She was offered a job in the Spencer Hotel, you know along the docks there?

ANNA. Yeah.

CORA. So…

ANNA. Right… good riddance.

CORA. Exactly.

ANNA (*beat*). *Was* that a year ago? Jesus…

CORA. Well, it was winter…

ANNA. It was.

CORA.…and it's winter now…

ANNA.…it feels like a couple of months at the most.

CORA. I know.

> *Pause.*

> And, c'mere: have you seen Denise at all? Or…

ANNA. Denise?

CORA. Yeah.

ANNA (*beat*). Sure what reason would I have to do that?

CORA. I dunno. I just thought, maybe…

ANNA. No.

CORA. Okay. (*Beat.*) No, I just thought, given how long it's been since I saw you, that, either of you…

ANNA. Right.

CORA.…that circumstances might have changed.

ANNA. Well, they haven't.

CORA. Okay.

ANNA. And they won't. So...

CORA. Right. No, fair enough.

Pause.

And do you never miss her?

ANNA. No, are you joking...?

CORA. No?

ANNA. ...I don't even think about her, Cora. Well, that's a lie. Now and again she'll come into my head and I'll feel a fleeting surge of fucking... rage or contempt or whatever. Hatred.

CORA. Right.

ANNA. But beyond that? No. She isn't someone who occupies my thoughts to any great extent.

Pause.

Why, when did *you* last see her?

CORA. Summer?

ANNA. Right.

CORA. We bumped into each other out in Dundrum.

ANNA. At the shopping centre?

CORA. Mm. (*Beat.*) She was giving out about you.

ANNA. Really.

CORA. Yeah.

ANNA. Over what?

CORA. The funeral?

ANNA. Why? Cos I didn't go?

CORA. Yeah.

ANNA. Give me a break. He wasn't *my* fucking boyfriend, was he? (*Beat.*) And *she* was there.

CORA. Huh?

ANNA. *She* was there. Any place *she* is, *I'm* not gonna be.

CORA. But, given, I dunno…

ANNA. Given what? (*Beat*.) How much I loved him?

CORA. Well, yeah.

ANNA. Will I tell you something, Cora? You've no idea.

CORA. Ah, I do.

ANNA. You…

CORA. Of course I do. Sure couldn't I see it every time I saw you together? Anyone could.

ANNA. Then why don't you understand my anger?

CORA. I do understand it. I just don't see, whatever, the benefit to it.

ANNA. There *is* no benefit to it.

CORA. Or the point.

ANNA. The point is, don't ever fuck someone over like that and expect there not to be consequences. He was the love of my fucking life, Cora.

CORA. I know.

ANNA. But, *do* you.

CORA. Yeah, sure I used to be so bloody jealous.

ANNA. Of what?

CORA. Of what you had. The intensity of it…

ANNA. It *was* intense.

CORA. …the way you always seemed so fucking tuned in to each other.

ANNA. Well, there you go. Then *she* comes along…

CORA. But that was *after* you'd broken up. See, this is why…

ANNA. Cora…

CORA. What?

ANNA (*beat*). Forget it.

CORA. It was, though.

ANNA. We hadn't broken up. And you *know* they were already fucking seeing each other…

CORA. I don't.

ANNA.…or were planning to at least. You do. And then one day, it's like, 'Anna, I need to talk to you…'

CORA. This is Oliver.

ANNA. Yes. '…about how unhappy I've been these last few…' Fucking bullshit!

CORA. Right.

ANNA. '…these last few months.' Bullshit! *He* lost interest in *me* because *she*…

CORA. But…

ANNA.…*she* fucking… What?

CORA. You don't know that.

ANNA. I do.

CORA. So, why does she tell it differently?

ANNA. That they met in Neary's? Give me a fucking…

CORA. Yes.

ANNA.…like, three weeks later? Give me a break, she was lying her arse off, Cora, and let me say this and I'll stop, cos this is a waste of time and I don't really want to discuss it in any case. But my love, that love you're talking about, that you were so envious of, was just as strong at the end for me as it was in those early days, all right? If not stronger. And that's the betrayal and that's the measure of it, and fuck Denise…

CORA. Okay.

ANNA.…and fuck Oliver too, and who cares if he fucking died? And you know what else? *I* have a man now who's loyal, who's kind and who loves me very much, and most importantly, there isn't a fucking, any *slut* around, who, of any man in the world to go after, wants to go after him, you know? (*Beat.*) Fucking bitch!

CORA. And who *is* he?

ANNA. Who?

CORA. This fella.

ANNA (*beat*). Did I not tell you?!

CORA. No.

ANNA. Oh, Cora! Sorry!

CORA. That's okay.

ANNA. So his name is Wayne…

CORA. Uh-huh.

ANNA.…he's from Cork… We're together, I dunno, about ten months now? Ten, eleven months?

CORA. And what does he do?

ANNA. He's in banking?

CORA. Right.

ANNA. Yeah, I know, but I'm mad about him, Cora. Like, really. I mean, it's not as intense or obsessive, now, as what I had with Oliver, which, you know, is a good thing, probably, given there's far less fuss…

CORA. Uh-huh.

ANNA.…or, whatever, conflict. Not that there was ever that *much*, but…

CORA. What is it, more mature? Or…

ANNA. Yeah, I suppose. Does that sound really fucking boring?

CORA. No.

ANNA. Cos he still makes my heart beat, Cora...

CORA. Does he?

ANNA. ...beat faster. Oh, he does, all right. And he can be *incredibly* romantic. You know what he did a few weeks ago? You won't believe this.

CORA. What did he do?

ANNA. He made this crossword...

CORA. What do you mean?

ANNA. Himself. Like, drew it, mapped out all the squares, the acrosses and downs, filled in the black bits, listed the clues. And the clues, or the answers to the clues...

CORA. This was for you to solve.

ANNA. That's right. And the answer to every clue was something intimate or romantic we'd done together, like...

CORA. Wow.

ANNA. ...all right?... like, one clue, say, would be 'Shrunken kidneys', and the answer...

CORA. 'Shrunken kidneys'?!

ANNA. Yeah, with a seven-letter answer, all right?

CORA. And what was it?

ANNA. Donegal...

CORA. Donegal?

ANNA. ...the clue, like, being a reference to when we were up there a while ago, and we went in the sea, and it was so, you know, cold we had to just stand there holding each other, and I was complaining my kidneys felt like they'd been shrunk to the size of, about, a pea.

CORA (*pause*). That's amazing.

ANNA. Isn't it?

CORA. No, I mean, Anna, that's *really* fucking romantic!

ANNA. Oh, Cora…

CORA. What?

ANNA.…I'm sorry. I forgot about, shit…

CORA. That's okay.

ANNA (*on 'okay'*).…about, no it's not. Here's me going on about my wonderful fucking relationship and…

CORA. Anna…

ANNA. No, but seriously. You've just gone through something absolutely horrendous, and…

CORA. Anna…

ANNA. What.

CORA.…stop. Just because things haven't gone great for me lately doesn't mean you're forbidden to talk about your life just because it's going well now. And you were so good to listen to all that anyway.

ANNA. Stop.

CORA. You were, though. The first time we see each other in God knows how long and here I am…

ANNA. Cora…

CORA.…no, but it's true, cataloguing my miseries for you.

ANNA. Sure who just finished ranting about her ex and her sister?!

CORA. Well…

ANNA. I was glad to listen, Cora.

CORA. Right. Well, it means a lot to me that you did. (*Beat.*) It's so helpful just to talk through this stuff, you know? So that, when you get down about it… because I do sometimes…

ANNA. Of course.

CORA. …I do… or wonder whether or not you've even made the right decision, there's someone, you know, outside of the situation…

ANNA. Someone objective.

CORA. Exactly… who's reassured you that what you're doing is right.

ANNA. Well, it is.

CORA. But…

ANNA. No, like, it *patently* is.

CORA. No, I know, but it's quite, you know, strengthening…

ANNA. Right.

CORA. …or empowering to be reminded of that. That's all. I mean, at the moment, I don't really have anybody I'm close enough to I'd feel in any way at ease discussing it with, you know?

ANNA. Really?

CORA. Yeah.

ANNA. Okay.

CORA. So, thank you.

ANNA. Well, listen: Any time.

CORA. Agh…

ANNA. I mean it, Cora. You know what, actually?

CORA. What?

ANNA. Do you not think it's kind of ridiculous how much time has passed each time we see each other?

CORA. I know.

ANNA. But, isn't it. I mean, we should meet more, far more often than we do.

CORA. That's true.

ANNA. Well, will we?

CORA. Yeah, sure…

ANNA. I mean, will you *call* me, or will *I* call *you*, say next week or something, and we'll go out for a drink, or, I dunno, a bite to eat, maybe?

CORA. Absolutely. No, I'd love that.

ANNA. So would I. I've loved *this*, actually.

CORA. Mm.

ANNA. Nice to have a bit of a moan on occasion.

CORA. Is that what we've been doing?

ANNA. Ah, Cora.

CORA. No, I suppose it is. (*Beat*.) Kind of reminds me of when the three of us used to live out in Ranelagh.

ANNA. Jesus.

CORA. Remember?

ANNA. Our celibate period.

CORA. We weren't *cel*ibate.

ANNA. What were we?

CORA. I dunno. We just weren't having much luck, I suppose.

ANNA. I suppose. (*Beat*.) Nice times, though.

CORA. McGuigan's.

ANNA. McGuigan's. God. (*Beat*.) Nicholas. What was his name?

CORA. The barman?

ANNA. Yeah.

CORA. That was it…

ANNA. Right.

CORA....Nicholas. No, they *were* nice times, all right. (*Beat.*) And then, sitting up till…

ANNA. True.

CORA....in the kitchen till all hours. Do you remember?

ANNA. Of course I remember. We didn't *only* moan, though, did we?

CORA. Ah, no. Sure we had a lot of fairly *deep* discussions, actually.

ANNA. Mm.

Pause.

CORA. Those nights really made an impression on me, though, you know that?

ANNA. Really?

CORA. Yeah.

ANNA. How?

CORA. I don't know. I just always kind of felt at the time we were so… The three of us, like…

ANNA. Uh-huh.

CORA....so in sync.

ANNA. In more ways than one.

CORA. Yeah, but… Hah! That's true. But, you know what I mean? The conversations were so…

ANNA. They were.

CORA....so intimate…

ANNA. Mm.

CORA....so passionate. *All* of us…

ANNA. Well, we were young, though.

CORA. I know, but…

ANNA. Young and naive.

CORA. …but I loved it. I mean, I *really* loved it. I mean, there were nights I didn't want it to end.

ANNA. Right.

CORA. It has a real, I have to say, just a special place in my… heart, I suppose, you know?

ANNA. Mm. No, I loved it too, Cora.

Silence.

Anyway…

CORA. What? You have to go?

ANNA. Yeah.

CORA. Oh, no!

ANNA. No, I know. (*As they stand.*) You have my number, don't you?

CORA. I do.

ANNA. And I have yours, so give me a call some time next week, or maybe the week after that, and…

CORA. I will.

ANNA. Or I'll call you. All right?

CORA. Cool.

ANNA. Excellent. (*As they embrace.*) I've loved doing this.

CORA. Me too.

ANNA. All right. Bye.

CORA. Bye.

ANNA *exits.*

CORA *sits back down.*

Entering:

DENISE. Sorry about that.

CORA. That's okay.

DENISE (*sitting down*). What was I saying?

CORA. Em… (*Beat.*) something about your shower. Oh, no…

DENISE. No, I said about my shower.

CORA. Your kitchen

DENISE. My counter…

CORA. Yes.

DENISE.…*in* my kitchen. That's right. Or my island, I mean. Okay, so, the morning they're putting it in, I'm out, I've a couple of things to do in town. So home I come, two or three o'clock, and they're done.

CORA. Okay.

DENISE. It's in, all right? But the bloody sink is wrong.

CORA. It's wrong?

DENISE. It isn't the one we ordered.

CORA. Right. Oh, no!

DENISE. We ordered the one with the marble draining board and they've put in the one with the metal one, right? No, I know. So I point this out to them, and the fucking resistance I get! 'Would you not just, since it's already in…?' All this shit. 'It'll take a whole 'nother day to replace it.' 'I don't give a fuck *how* long it takes, it isn't what we asked for!'

CORA. God.

DENISE.…you know? Or, more importantly, paid for.

CORA. So *did* they replace it?

DENISE. You're fucking right they did. But they hated me, Cora.

CORA. Did they?

DENISE. Ah, yeah. I hung around most of the following day and, every time I walked in, I could feel them...

CORA. Right.

DENISE....to the kitchen, like...

CORA. Their resentment.

DENISE. Exactly. 'Fucking bitch!'

CORA. And...

DENISE. 'Battleaxe!'

CORA. And otherwise did they do a good job?

DENISE. Oh, they did, they did a fantastic job with everything else. But that's just it. It all gets tarnished right at the end over, what? Laziness. Or...

CORA. Right.

DENISE....I dunno. Just not *giving* a shit, I suppose. Oh, but you have to see it, Cora!

CORA. The sink?

DENISE. Well, yeah, well, the whole extension. I mean, if you'd seen the kitchen before, which I know you haven't, but it was a poke! And filthy...!

CORA. Uh-huh.

DENISE....but tiny as well, and now we have this living space, this huge... Well, not huge, but big, you know?... this relaxing area which, yeah. I mean, yeah. I mean, we're so happy with it.

CORA. What's his name again?

DENISE. Gerard? Who?

CORA. Your husband.

DENISE. Gerard.

CORA. And Conor's your baby.

DENISE. He's at his nana's today, giving me a break, which is much appreciated. And much needed, I have to say.

CORA. Why, is it tough?

DENISE. Is what tough? Being a mother?

CORA. Mm.

DENISE. It's tough enough, to be honest, yeah. And, I mean, he's a wonderful child. He isn't a crier, you know, or colicky or anything else like that, but, still, however well behaved a baby is, it's, yeah, it's still difficult, Cora. I mean, really. And tiring.

CORA. Okay.

DENISE. And constant. You don't get a break.

CORA. Except for today.

DENISE. Well, except for the odd day Gerard's mother takes him. She's nice, so…

CORA. Is she?

DENISE. Ah, yeah. Totally not, you know, the cliché or whatever. And Conor's her only grandchild, so she really dotes on him, which is lovely. But you don't want to be taking advantage either, you know?

CORA. No, of course. (*Beat*.) And *what* does Gerard do?

DENISE. He's a graphic designer.

CORA. Oh, right. That's a decent job, is it not?

DENISE. No, it is. I mean, he's freelance, so sometimes he has to wait for the work?

CORA. To be offered it.

DENISE. Yeah, so it can be a bit precarious that way. But when things are going well, which they are at the moment, thank God, then you're kind of flying. Hence, I mean…

CORA. Right.

DENISE.…the new extension, et cetera.

Long pause.

CORA. What?

DENISE. Can I tell you something else?

CORA. Go on.

DENISE. I'm pregnant again.

CORA. No!

DENISE. Three months. Or just over, actually.

CORA. God! Denise!

DENISE. I know. It's so soon after Conor, but time is short, given…

CORA. Absolutely.

DENISE.…given my age. There are far more risks. I mean, his birth was traumatic enough in the first place, so…

CORA. Was it?

DENISE. Mm.

CORA. How?

DENISE. Well, they tell you, they monitor you, you know? Or not you, but the baby. Well, you *and* the baby, and it was all going fine, I was four, like, centimetres dilated, but then they kind of panicked a bit?

CORA. Who's 'they'?

DENISE. The midwife…

CORA. Right.

DENISE.…some other guy. I dunno.

CORA. The obstetrician?

DENISE. No, he was off.

CORA. He was off?!

DENISE. Yeah.

CORA. Where?

DENISE. On holiday. Don't even start me on that. But they said he was getting, the baby, like, was getting distressed in there.

CORA. What's that?

DENISE. Distressed?

CORA. Yeah.

DENISE. His heartbeat was going too fast. So, they had to rush me into an operating room and give me a cesarean.

CORA. Wow.

DENISE. And Gerard was thrown out too.

CORA. Really?

DENISE. Mm.

CORA. I thought the man could watch a caesarean.

DENISE. Not if it's an emergency…

CORA. Oh.

DENISE.…like, if they have to put you under.

CORA. Did they put you under?

DENISE. The epidural wasn't taking. That was another thing. You know the epidural.

CORA. Yes.

DENISE. I still had feeling down in my lower half, so they had to.

CORA. God.

DENISE. So I never got to, me *or* Gerard, actually, ever got to witness this special, you know, this sacred event in our lives.

CORA. Oh, that's terrible.

DENISE. Agh…

CORA. What.

DENISE....I don't care, you know what? I did for a short while, actually, but then you just think, 'He's here, he's in our lives, so it doesn't really matter how he arrived or whether we witnessed it or not.' Anyway, this time they say we have to go straight to the section, which, again, I'm not completely happy about. But, listen...

CORA....if that's the safest way...

DENISE. Exactly.

CORA (*beat*). Wow.

DENISE (*beat*). What.

CORA. Just 'Wow'. Who'd ever have thought your life, you know, would have turned out like this.

DENISE. I'm really happy, Cora.

CORA. I can see that. And, I mean, after such a...

DENISE (*beat*). What?

CORA....a devastation.

DENISE. Oliver?

CORA. Yeah.

DENISE. You know what? Can I say something?

CORA. Yeah, of course.

DENISE. I mean, Oliver... (*Pause.*) when he died, I *was* fairly broken up.

CORA. I know.

DENISE....you remember? But, to be honest, I... (*Beat.*) I'm not sure I ever really loved him, Cora.

CORA (*beat*). Okay.

DENISE. Is that awful? And, you know, that doesn't mean my grief wasn't genuine, but a part of it, I think, is probably, how should I put it...? (*Beat.*) was me kinda playing the *part* of the devastated partner?

CORA. Right.

DENISE. Is that terrible, Cora?

CORA. No, not at all. I just…

DENISE. What?

CORA. …I just never knew.

DENISE. Well, that's kind of what was expected of me, you see, and…

CORA. Right.

DENISE. …and, you know? I mean, wasn't it?

CORA. Yeah, I suppose.

DENISE. …and I *did* feel terrible. Of course, and my tears *were* real, but they weren't really proper, like, grieving tears, cos there wasn't… I mean, to be honest, I'm not too sure, if he'd lived, whether we would have stayed together much longer in *any* case, you know?

CORA. Okay.

DENISE. And I know that must be shocking to you, Cora…

CORA. Well…

DENISE. No, I know, but it's only now, you see, that I've something real to, real and deep to compare it to. And lasting…

CORA. Gerard, you mean.

DENISE. Yeah… and honest, the slight, you know, shallowness, I suppose, of what me and Oliver had is just…

CORA (*beat*). It's exposed.

DENISE. It is, yeah.

CORA. Right.

DENISE. It is. I mean, with Gerard… (*Beat.*) I dunno. Whatever. I'm rabbiting on.

CORA. No, that's fine.

DENISE. No, I am. Tell me something else about you.

CORA. Like what?

DENISE. How's work?

CORA. Work's fine. I'm still in Corrigan's.

DENISE. Right.

CORA. ...For my sins.

DENISE. 'For your sins.' It isn't *that* bad, is it? Actually, whatever happened with that one you were saying?

CORA. Fiona?

DENISE. Was that her name?

CORA. Who used to be at me?

DENISE. Yeah.

CORA. Fiona. Yeah, she left…

DENISE. She left?!

CORA. ...she's gone a couple of years now, actually.

DENISE. Bitch. She was jealous of you, you know that?

CORA. Yeah, no, Anna said something similar.

DENISE. Did she?

CORA. Mm.

DENISE. Well, there you go, you know? I mean, if two of us think it…

CORA. No, that's true.

Beat.

DENISE. So, what else?

CORA. What else? (*Beat.*) Bridie died…

DENISE. She didn't die! When?!

CORA. Fairly recently, actually.

DENISE. Cora!

CORA. Mm. I mean, she was very old, now…

DENISE. I know, but you must have been devastated, were you?

CORA. Devastated enough, yeah.

DENISE. God! Oh, I'm sorry to hear that, darling!

CORA. Listen: she was a dog.

DENISE. Still, though.

CORA. No, I know.

DENISE. And, c'mere: would you and Anna see each other a lot, so?

CORA. Me and Anna?!

DENISE. Yeah.

CORA. God, no, sure the last time I spoke to Anna was…

DENISE. Right.

CORA. …a good while back.

DENISE (*beat*). And how was she?

CORA. Yeah, she was fine.

DENISE. Okay.

CORA. Actually, no. She'd just just broken up with a guy she was seeing, so she was a bit depressed.

DENISE. Who was he?

CORA. I dunno. His name, like?

DENISE. Yeah.

CORA. Wayne something? I never got to meet him, but they were going out a good long while, I think. A year and a half, something like that? He was offered a job somewhere and she didn't want to go with him…

DENISE. Abroad, like?

CORA. Yeah.

DENISE. And *he* wouldn't stay for *her*?

CORA. Well, he didn't.

DENISE. Jesus. They can't have been *that* fucking mad about one another, then, can they?

CORA. I don't know. The previous time I saw her, when they were still together, she said that he was the, seriously…

DENISE. The one?

CORA. The one.

DENISE. Right.

CORA. …seriously. You would have expected, the way she was going on, or I would've anyway, that they'd have been married next time, like yourself, with a baby or whatever, the next, like, time I saw her, but no…

DENISE. No.

CORA. …back to the drawing board.

DENISE. Back to the, right. Well, it takes, I suppose, a crisis of some sort sometimes, or an upheaval, for people to really evaluate how they feel about one another, doesn't it?

CORA. Yeah, I suppose.

DENISE. And how long ago was this?

CORA. Five, six months? The *last* time I saw her?

DENISE. Yeah.

CORA. Yeah, about five, six months. I ran into her in the Jervis Centre.

DENISE. Right.

Long pause.

CORA. I can't get over the length of your hair!

DENISE. Is it better, though?

CORA. Yes!

DENISE. Are you sure?

CORA. Ah, it's gorgeous, Denise. I mean, it was beautiful short as well, but…

DENISE. Right.

CORA. …I dunno. You had it that way for so long…

DENISE. Since Ranelagh.

CORA. Really?

DENISE. Yeah, sure that's where I first got it cut.

CORA. Oh, that's right!

DENISE. The Paris Salon.

CORA. That's right.

DENISE. So, when did we last see each other?

CORA. About three years ago.

DENISE. Really? No, it would be, wouldn't it. God.

Pause.

The Paris Salon.

CORA. Mm.

DENISE. Stan. What was his name?

CORA. Stan?!

DENISE. Yeah.

CORA. Stuart!

DENISE. Oh, of course. (*Beat.*) Stuart.

CORA. Our celibate period.

DENISE. Mm.

CORA. Or was it just that we weren't having much luck?

DENISE. We were on a hiatus.

CORA. Is that what it was?

DENISE. A sabbatical.

CORA. That's right. That's what we were on. (*Beat*.) Though, you know what? I have to say that that was a very important time in my life. (*Beat*.) I mean, really.

DENISE. Right.

CORA. I mean, a time that, the older I get, the more it seems to mean to me, you know?

DENISE. The memory of it?

CORA. Yeah.

DENISE. No, I do.

CORA. All that time we spent together. Those conversations. And I know a lot of what we talked about was nonsense, but...

DENISE. We were such fucking moaners.

CORA. Weren't we?

DENISE. Although, no...

CORA. What?

DENISE. ...no, I mean, *some* of it was nonsense, but we had a lot of good chats too.

CORA. We did. (*Beat*.) Deep.

DENISE. Hm?

CORA. Deep chats.

DENISE. ...Didn't we?

CORA. That's what I mean, though. The closeness the three of us had, the intimacy or whatever. I really consider it, like, a special, a formative part of my life...

DENISE. Uh-huh.

CORA. ...a cherished part. I dunno.

DENISE. No, it was pretty special for all of us, I'd say.

Long pause.

CORA. Would you not ever think about…?

DENISE. What?

CORA.…you know, getting in touch. Or…

DENISE. With Anna?!

CORA. Yeah.

DENISE. Fuck her, why should I? Because she's unhappy?

CORA. Well, because he's gone.

DENISE. Who, Oliver?

CORA. Yeah.

DENISE. Oliver's gone a *long* time, Cora, and what the hell has he got to do with it, anyway?

CORA. Well, he's the source of her anger.

DENISE. No.

CORA. He isn't?

DENISE. He was.

CORA. Well, that's what I'm saying…

DENISE. Right.

CORA.…he's dead now.

DENISE. But he wasn't the only one she was angry *at*. *Is* angry at. And fuck her anger anyway, Cora, what about mine?

CORA. Your anger?

DENISE. I'm the one who was wrongly accused, who was punished, so what about *my* fucking righteous indignation? What about *my* fucking hurt? Shutting me out of her life over something she fucking *assumed* happened between me and him. *Assumed*…

CORA. Well…

DENISE. ...*Decided* happened between us.

CORA. But it hadn't.

DENISE. Huh?

CORA. It hadn't happened.

DENISE. Are you asking me or telling me?

CORA (*beat*). I...

DENISE. Cos you've asked me before and I've answered and I've answered truthfully, Cora, so what I said then isn't gonna change now.

CORA. You weren't seeing each other.

DENISE. Why are you asking me?

CORA. I'm not.

DENISE. You are!

CORA. Well...

DENISE. No. We weren't fucking seeing each other. We'd no interest in each other till after *their* thing ended, till we met that night in Neary's, then that subsequent night in the, look: I'm not gonna try and convince you, Cora...

CORA. No...

DENISE. ...of the facts.

CORA. No, I am convinced, Denise.

DENISE. Then you know that I was the wronged one in this.

CORA. I do.

DENISE. Not her.

CORA. Okay. And so...

DENISE. All right?

CORA. No, okay. Absolutely okay. And so, say if she was to come to you...

DENISE. Right.

CORA....to apologise, would you... (*Beat*.)

DENISE. What? Accept it?

CORA. Yeah.

DENISE. No, I wouldn't.

CORA. Why not?

DENISE. Because there was a death. And someone was grieving. And that grieving someone needed someone to comfort her, but that someone didn't care to, Cora, she preferred to continue to punish instead, and I'll *never* forgive her that, can you understand?

CORA. But you said that you didn't care for him at the end.

DENISE. I cared for him, Cora.

CORA. But that you weren't upset.

DENISE. I wasn't *that* upset, but I was fucking upset.

CORA. Okay.

DENISE....you know? And Anna would have assumed I was in any case.

CORA. Very upset.

DENISE. Yeah, like, devastated, and that her absence would have hurt far worse than it actually did. And it *did*.

CORA. Right.

DENISE. Of *course* it did. But worse. So she knew *exactly* what she was doing, Cora.

CORA. Punishing you.

DENISE. Exactly. But to a hateful fucking degree. And anyone who'd do something like that, I mean, to her sister, and I don't give a damn what she imagined happened, is someone that sister's better off having out of her life. That was a line that she crossed, okay? And that there'll never be any turning back from.

Long pause.

CORA. And is it an issue ever with, em…

DENISE.…Do you understand?

CORA. No, I do.

DENISE. Is it an issue ever with who? With Gerard?

CORA. Yeah.

DENISE. It's not an 'issue'…

CORA. Right.

DENISE.…it's something we've discussed. The whole idea of Conor having an aunt he'll never see or whatever. But every family has an estrangement somewhere in there, doesn't it?

CORA. I suppose.

DENISE.…Of some sort.

CORA. And is he understanding that way?

DENISE. Gerard?

CORA. Mm.

DENISE. Ah, he is. I'm really happy, Cora.

CORA. Great.

DENISE. Like, seriously. (*Beat.*) But, c'mere: you must be as well.

CORA. I must be?

DENISE. Or excited at least. Well, yeah, well, what about *your* fella?

CORA. What about him?

DENISE. *You* tell *me*.

CORA. Agh. (*Beat.*) I suddenly feel like my love life's completely adolescent next to yours.

DENISE. What?!

CORA. Yeah. Or stunted.

DENISE. Listen: you could argue there's no adventure in mine any more.

CORA. Nor should there be at your age.

DENISE. Right.

CORA. Or mine. Which is the bloody problem.

DENISE. Come on. You're going out a month…

CORA. Well, we actually went out before.

DENISE. Oh, really?! When?

CORA. A couple of years ago.

DENISE. I never met him, though.

CORA. No.

DENISE. Okay. And why'd you break up? Or is that not something you wanna…

CORA. No, not at all… to talk about?

DENISE. Yeah.

CORA. No, sure I'm happy to talk about it, I just… There was no specific reason, really…

DENISE. Right.

CORA. …or event, we just kind of never connected properly. Like, the circumstances were wrong, or…

DENISE. How?

CORA. …or the timing… How?

DENISE. Uh-huh.

CORA. I don't know. Like, neither of us was probably in the right, like, place in our lives, I don't think, in terms of maturity, say, or emotionally, or whatever.

DENISE. Right. That can happen.

CORA. …you know? So we argued a lot.

DENISE. Over what?

CORA. Jesus, you name it. Although we were very passionate too.

DENISE. Why don't I *know* about any of this?! Go on.

CORA. Well, I haven't seen you, Denise.

DENISE. I know. Go on. What else?

CORA. Nothing else. In the end, we just decided it wasn't really worth it any more.

DENISE. And how long had you been together?

CORA. A year…?

DENISE. Okay.

CORA. …maybe a little bit more than that? Anyway, so about six weeks ago, maybe, we ran into each other up around Grand Canal Dock and went for a coffee and kind of got on, so we met again a couple of times, and we're sort of, I think we are, anyway, sort of going to give it another go.

DENISE. Good for you.

CORA. Mm.

DENISE (*beat*). And does it feel different this time round?

CORA. I think so, yeah, because…

DENISE. Right…

CORA. …*we're* different.

DENISE (*simultaneously*). …*you're* different.

CORA. Exactly. Everything just feels more kind of attuned now.

DENISE. Well, time will do that, won't it?

CORA. No, it will. It will.

DENISE. I can tell you're mad about him.

CORA. How?

DENISE. I just can. Go on.

CORA. That's all.

DENISE. No it's not. What else? Is he very romantic?

CORA. He is, yeah.

DENISE. Tell me something romantic he's done.

CORA. Why?

DENISE. Cos I'm interested. (*Beat*.) Would he buy you flowers?

CORA. Ah, yeah.

DENISE. What else?

CORA. Em… (*Beat*.) *I* don't know.

DENISE. So, he isn't really.

CORA. What?

DENISE. Romantic.

CORA. He is, I just… (*Beat*.) See, you're putting pressure on.

DENISE. All right. Sorry.

CORA. No, just… (*Beat*.) All right.

DENISE. What.

CORA. Okay. I'll tell you something he did. (*Beat*.) He made me this crossword…

DENISE. Right.

CORA. …like, drew it.

DENISE. Drew it.

CORA. Yeah, like, with all the boxes and all the clues. Cryptic clues, really clever, like, and the answer to each was something me and him had done together when we first went out.

DENISE. What do you mean? Oh, wow!

CORA. …right?

DENISE. Really?!

CORA. Something romantic, yeah.

DENISE. Like what, though?

CORA. Well, like, say, there was one, let me think… (*Beat.*) All right, so one, for example, said, 'After *The Graduate*', and it was, three, five, four…

DENISE. Letters.

CORA. Sorry?

DENISE. They were the…

CORA. Yeah. Three words…

DENISE. Right.

CORA. …Three, five, four, and the answer was, 'Our first time', because…

DENISE. 'Our first time.'

CORA. …because, yeah. Because, the first time we ever did it, like, slept together, it was in his place after we watched that movie.

DENISE (*pause*). Oh, Cora!

CORA. What.

DENISE. That's *very* romantic!

CORA. Is it?

DENISE. Oh, it is! Oh, you've got to hang on to him!

CORA. I know. (*Beat.*) I actually don't think I've ever felt this way about someone.

DENISE. Really?

CORA. Mm.

DENISE. Even Ciaran?

CORA. Ciaran. Jesus. No, though, Ciaran, I don't think, even came close.

DENISE. Wow.

CORA. Mm.

DENISE. Sure you know what...? What's his name again?

CORA. Noah.

DENISE. Right.

CORA. That's fine. Just think of the Ark.

DENISE. Yeah, exactly. But, listen: why don't you and him come over for dinner?

CORA. When?

DENISE. I dunno. Like, soon.

CORA. Yeah, I mean...

DENISE. Yeah? Cos I'd love to meet him. And for you to meet Gerard and Conor, of course.

CORA. No, that'd be brilliant, Denise.

DENISE. Well, will we do that, then?

CORA. Absolutely.

DENISE. Excellent.

Long pause.

CORA. Anyway...

DENISE. What? You have to go?

CORA. Yeah.

DENISE. Oh, no!

CORA. No, I know.

DENISE (*as they stand*). Well, it was great to see you.

CORA. Oh, you too, Denise! (*As they embrace*.) And congratulations again on your pregnancy.

DENISE. Oh...

CORA. It's fantastic news.

DENISE.…Thanks. Give me a call now, won't you? And we'll arrange a date.

CORA. I will.

DENISE. Or I'll call you. You're on the same number, are you?

CORA. Yeah.

DENISE. Me too.

CORA. Okay. Talk to you then.

DENISE. Bye.

CORA. Bye.

She exits.

DENISE *sits back down.*

Entering:

ANNA. Sorry about that.

DENISE. That's okay. (*Beat.*) You were saying.

ANNA (*sitting down*). What was I saying? Oh, right…

DENISE. The architecture.

ANNA.…That's right. Oh, Denise! I mean, even for someone, you know, with no interest in that kind of thing. Little narrow streets leading onto squares with outdoor cafés and all these beautiful churches everywhere. Well, not everywhere, but, you know…

DENISE. There were a lot of them.

ANNA. Or a fair few, yeah. And the place I was staying was over one of the main squares, so every morning I'd go down to the bakery on the corner and buy myself a croissant and coffee, then go back up then and have them out on my balcony, sit there looking down at all the locals, whatever…

DENISE. Right.

ANNA.…the tourists…

DENISE. And were you not a bit lonely being there on your own?

ANNA. Not really.

DENISE. Or bored, or…

ANNA. No, sure that kind of added to it a bit, I'd say, in that I was kind of master of my own destiny. Like, I…

DENISE. Right.

ANNA.…you know, could get up when I wanted, go to the beach when I wanted, eat when I wanted…

DENISE. And were the Italians nice?

ANNA. Sicilians.

DENISE. Sorry.

ANNA. Yeah, I dunno. I mean, I didn't talk to many.

DENISE. And what about fellas?

ANNA. What?

DENISE. Did you have any coming on to you?

ANNA. Me…?!

DENISE. Yeah.

ANNA.…No. Sure, what bloody interest would they have in me?

DENISE. Plenty, Anna.

ANNA. Denise…

DENISE. Come on.

ANNA. At my age? *You* come on. With *my* fucking pasty Irish body?

DENISE. You've a fantastic body.

ANNA. Yeah, right.

DENISE. You do, and would paleness not, you know, make you exotic to them?

ANNA. Well, it didn't. So…

DENISE. Right. Well, *I* think you look incredible, Anna. Seriously. *And* you've a real, I don't know, a *healthy* glow off you.

ANNA. Really?

DENISE. Yeah.

ANNA. No, a *couple* of people have said that, actually.

DENISE. ...or contented, you know?

ANNA. Well, that's the kind of place it *is*, I suppose. Or the part I went to anyway.

DENISE. What was it called again?

ANNA. Cefalu.

DENISE. Cefalu. And what made you pick, like, there specifically?

ANNA. Well, that's where Mam went.

DENISE. What?

ANNA. And Dad. (*Beat.*) Do you not remember?

DENISE. No.

ANNA. Ah, you do, Denise. When Angela minded us.

DENISE. Back in primary school!

ANNA. Yes.

DENISE. Oh, is that where they went that time?!

ANNA. And I felt... Yeah...

DENISE. I see!

ANNA. ...and I felt, I dunno, I was going away in any case, and I just thought it might be nice to experience something special that *they* experienced.

DENISE. Ah, Anna...

ANNA. What?

DENISE....I'd fucking love to have done that with you!

ANNA. Yeah, but...

DENISE. No, I know. I know. (*Beat*.) Still.

ANNA. Well, maybe one day we could go back together.

DENISE. Yeah, that'd be amazing.

Long pause.

I had a dream about her the other night.

ANNA. Who?

DENISE. Mam.

ANNA. Okay.

DENISE. No, we just... I was sitting on a bench with her in a park... You remember the one behind Fox's?

ANNA. Uh-huh.

DENISE. In there. And she was telling me I had to take Gerard back for the sake of the kids, and in the dream I had four instead of just Conor, and they were running around in the grass, two boys and two girls, and she was going on about how a child without a dad'll have an unbalanced upbringing and won't have, you know, the male, the essential...

ANNA. Right.

DENISE....male guidance.

ANNA. Which is nonsense.

DENISE....or influence.

ANNA. Which is nonsense, though.

DENISE. Sure I know it is.

ANNA. And what then?

DENISE. That was it.

ANNA. That was it?

DENISE. Mm-hm.

ANNA. Weird.

DENISE. I know.

Pause.

ANNA. And *would* you take him back?

DENISE. You must be joking. Jesus. (*Beat.*) Do you know your woman lives not far from me?

ANNA. Who? She doesn't!

DENISE. Uh-huh.

ANNA. They're not still together, though.

DENISE. *No*, no...

ANNA. Right.

DENISE. ...No, that's over a *good* while now. But I see her in Tesco, down on the main road...

ANNA. Really?

DENISE. Yeah, or say if I'm coming out of the butcher's or wherever with Conor, I have to, we both do, actually, have to stare straight ahead...

ANNA. You and Conor?

DENISE. No, me and her.

ANNA. Oh, right.

DENISE. ...as if each of us doesn't know who the other is.

ANNA. Shit.

DENISE. Mm.

ANNA. That's awkward. (*Beat.*) And how *is* Conor?

DENISE. Yeah, he's fantastic.

ANNA. Is he? And is he gorgeous?

DENISE. Well, you'll have to see him, Anna.

ANNA. I know.

DENISE. But, yeah. He is. Although now that it's only the two of us, I have to say, it's fairly tough. I mean, not that I can imagine not having him in my life. Jesus, God forbid. But, *thank* God, at the same time, we didn't have two, let alone...

ANNA. Two kids?

DENISE. ...yeah, let alone four, you know?

ANNA. Why four?

DENISE. Cos that's what I had in the dream.

ANNA. Oh, right. Yeah.

Pause.

I've dreamt about *you*.

DENISE. Really?

ANNA. A good few times.

DENISE. Well, *I've* dreamt about *you* a few times.

ANNA. No, you haven't.

DENISE. I have, yeah. What would *you* dream?

ANNA. That we were shopping.

DENISE. Right.

ANNA. Or sometimes swimming.

DENISE. Where? In the sea?

ANNA. No, at the pool in Balrothery.

DENISE. Right. I had one, you had a motorbike and you wouldn't give me a go.

ANNA. A motorbike?!

DENISE. Yeah.

ANNA. That's weird.

DENISE. Or a scooter, you know, like a moped?

ANNA. Yeah.

DENISE. It *was* weird. And it was me and Emily Dowling…

ANNA. Who?!

DENISE. From school. *You* remember…

ANNA. Yeah. No, I'm just saying, 'God…!'

DENISE. Right.

ANNA. '…Of all the people!'

DENISE. I know. But, anyway, I was terrified, like, genuinely, like disproportionately, that you'd give her a go before me.

ANNA. Why?

DENISE. Huh?

ANNA. Why were you terrified?

DENISE. I don't know.

ANNA. And did I?

DENISE. I couldn't say. I woke up before the bloody thing ended.

ANNA. Okay.

Pause.

Did I ever tell you I met her mother one day, there, three or four years ago?

DENISE. Emily's?

ANNA. Yeah.

DENISE. Where?

ANNA. In town.

DENISE. Right. (*Beat.*) And did you talk to her?

ANNA. No, not really. We just said hello to each other. I remember she looked really awful, though.

DENISE. What do you mean?

ANNA. Just really old…

DENISE. Okay.

ANNA.…and worn.

DENISE. Well, I suppose, with the level of grief I'm sure she's been dealing with all these years. I mean, could you imagine?

ANNA. Mm.

DENISE. Your child? I mean, the very *idea* of losing Conor'd age me, Anna, let alone if it actually happened, you know? (*Beat.*) So cute. He comes in at, let me tell you this, to my room at night, he wakes and gets in beside me.

ANNA. Does he?

DENISE. Yeah, and I shouldn't let him, you know? But…

ANNA. Why?

DENISE. Well, cos it'll teach him bad habits, or so they say, but what the hell can I do? It's just the two of us there and he's scared and he needs his mammy, I'm hardly gonna send him back to his room.

ANNA. And what bad habits would it teach him?

DENISE. Well, that *is* the bad habit, I suppose. I don't want, nine or ten years old, he's still coming in to me, you know? You also hear people say it'll make him a mammy's boy…

ANNA. Or give him an Oedipal complex.

DENISE. Jesus, stop! (*Beat.*) No, but, for the moment, I just couldn't bear to send him away.

ANNA (*beat*). And do you ever get lonely?

DENISE. What do you mean?

ANNA. You know…

DENISE. Yeah, now and again, I suppose. But, I dunno, these days, the idea of even going out on a date exhausts me, let alone, you know, all the complications of, whatever…

ANNA. Right. A relationship.

DENISE. Exactly. Although I do miss sex.

ANNA. I don't.

DENISE. Do you not? How long is it since *you've* been with someone?

ANNA. Nearly a year, I'd say.

DENISE. A year?

ANNA. Yeah. Maybe more than that.

DENISE. Wow.

ANNA. Mm. And, I mean, I can't say I haven't been lonely as well at times, cos I have. But I just… Well, it's the same as *you're* saying. I just can't be arsed engaging with all the *emotional* nonsense. And I'm including the highs in that by the way…

DENISE. Uh-huh.

ANNA.…the euphoria or whatever. It just depresses me at the moment even to think about that stuff, you know? (*Beat.*) And, of course, with my track record lately…

DENISE. Well, you've had a lot of disappointments.

ANNA. I have. I mean, not that *you* haven't! Jesus…

DENISE. Tell me about it.

ANNA. But, yeah. I have to admit, this last while, I'm really enjoying being on my own.

DENISE. Hence…

ANNA. Right.

DENISE.…your holiday.

ANNA. Well, exactly. Cos my head isn't filled with things it doesn't need to be filled with, and I can think now, and, you know what? It doesn't have to be forever. I might change my mind in six months' time, I might change my mind next week, and I reserve the right to do either, by the way…

DENISE. Okay. But for now…

ANNA. For now, I couldn't be happier, really. Well, not happier…

DENISE. More content.

ANNA. …more comfortable, we'll say…

DENISE. Okay.

ANNA. …in my day-to-day, you know…

DENISE. Existence.

ANNA (*on 'Existence'*). I'll tell you what I'm happy about… Existence. Exactly.

DENISE. What are you happy about?

ANNA. You being back in my life?

DENISE (*beat*). Anna…

ANNA. Seriously.

DENISE. I know. Sure I feel the same way. I mean, what were we thinking? What was *I* thinking?

ANNA. No, me as well.

DENISE. So stupid.

ANNA. Mm.

DENISE. So idiotic.

ANNA. No, me as well, you know? I remember one time, actually, chatting to Cora…

DENISE. Cora. Jesus.

ANNA. Yeah, I know.

Pause.

DENISE. Go on, though.

ANNA. Well…

DENISE. You were chatting and…

ANNA. Yeah, about when we used to live in Ranelagh…

DENISE. Right.

ANNA.…and…

DENISE. Those were amazing days.

ANNA. Well, that's…

DENISE.…I mean, weren't they?

ANNA. Absolutely. Well, that's what I'm saying. I remember I got quite emotional.

DENISE. Really.

ANNA. Yeah.

DENISE. Why?

ANNA. Cos I missed you.

DENISE. Gimme a break.

ANNA. No, I did, Denise. I did. And just talking all about that stuff, those days, it really, you know, kind of brought it home to me.

DENISE. Brought what home?

ANNA. I don't know. Your absence. Cos we were so bloody close then.

DENISE. Mm.

ANNA.…I mean, weren't we?

DENISE. Well, cos we spent all our time together.

ANNA. You know what I loved?

DENISE. The kitchen table…?

ANNA. Yeah, but…

DENISE.…sitting up until all hours?

ANNA. No, that was good, all right, but you know what I *really* loved? Like, you know what's always had, like, a really special place in my heart? (*Beat.*) Kennedy's.

DENISE. Ah…!

ANNA. On…

DENISE.… Yes!

ANNA. On Saturday mornings.

DENISE. Scrambled eggs and toast.

ANNA. That's right.

DENISE. *That* was special.

ANNA. And rashers.

DENISE. Just you and me.

ANNA. That's right. It *was* special.

DENISE (*beat*). The window seat.

ANNE. I hated when we'd walk in and there'd be someone already there.

DENISE. No, me too.

ANNA. I remember, actually…

DENISE (*on 'actually'*). We'd be so disappointed.

ANNA. Mm.

DENISE. What do you remember?

ANNA. Agh… It's sentimental.

DENISE. I don't care. Go on.

ANNA. Just one morning, the sun was shining in, we were *at* the table…

DENISE. Right. The window…

ANNA. Yeah. And you were just sitting there, staring into space, and I just thought…

DENISE. What?

ANNA.… 'Has she any idea how gorgeous she is?'

DENISE. Fuck off.

ANNA. No, I'm serious, Denise.

DENISE. Well, maybe *then* I was.

ANNA. No, still.

DENISE. 'Still' what?

ANNA. You still have a bit of majesty to you.

DENISE. 'A bit of majesty'! (*Beat*.) Oh, Anna.

ANNA. I know.

DENISE. We're birds of a fucking feather, aren't we?

ANNA. Yeah.

DENISE. So easily hurt.

ANNA. And quick to cut off our noses to spite our faces.

DENISE. Mm.

Long pause.

ANNA. It's weird. You know, you look back and you wonder...
(*Beat*.) Okay, I'm gonna be honest here.

DENISE. Is this about Oliver?

ANNA. Yeah. Unless you don't wanna...

DENISE. No, that's all right.

ANNA. Are you sure?

DENISE. Yeah.

ANNA. All right. Well... (*Beat*.) I'm not really sure if I ever
loved him all that *much*, Denise. (*Beat*.) I mean, I thought
I did, I suppose, but... (*Beat*.) I dunno, I mean, Jesus, the
way we'd be all over each other, you know? Always...

DENISE. Mm.

ANNA. You remember?

DENISE. Absolutely.

ANNA.…Always drawing attention to the fact that we were a couple and how mad we were about each other. And physically, I suppose we were, but beyond that, I'm just not sure there was that much *there*, Denise. And then, of course, over time, you get to the point where the physical thing isn't really enough any more, and you kind of, or we did, anyway, become two people who just get on, like, who are fond of each other, but, you know…

DENISE.…No more than that.

ANNA. Exactly.

DENISE. Right. (*Pause*.) So, why did you get so angry?

ANNA. When he broke up with me?

DENISE. Yes.

ANNA. Or when he and you got together? Pride…?

DENISE. Right.

ANNA.…Ego? I don't know. It was you I was angry at more than him, though. Probably bec…

DENISE. Really.

ANNA. Yes.

DENISE. Why?

ANNA. Well, because I probably felt there was some sort of rule there.

DENISE. Rule about what?

ANNA. About sisters. I dunno, about ownership or… (*Beat*.) I dunno. I was wrong, of course.

DENISE. No, you weren't really.

ANNA. I wasn't?

DENISE. Not really. Well, there probably *is* a rule, and I probably *should've* asked permission, or…

ANNA. No…

DENISE....or... 'No'?

ANNA....sure why should you have to do that? See, that's what I'm saying...

DENISE. Well, at least I should have talked to you after I met him that first time, instead of leaving it till...

ANNA. Mm.

DENISE....till we were already...

ANNA. Well, *that* hurt.

DENISE. Right.

ANNA. And that's, I suppose, what made me suspicious about, you know, whether something had *already* been going on.

DENISE. Before you broke up.

ANNA. Yeah.

DENISE. I know, but it's one of those things, you dread the conversation, and so you put it off, and you put it off...

ANNA. I get you.

DENISE....and then...

ANNA. It becomes too late.

DENISE. It does.

ANNA. And did *you* love him?

DENISE (*pause*). The truth?

ANNA. Of course.

DENISE (*beat*). Yes.

ANNA. Oh, Denise...

DENISE. Very much.

ANNA....I'm so sorry. And me not there to support you after he died...

DENISE. Listen...

ANNA....and not willing to even come to the...

DENISE. Anna...

ANNA....the funeral, fucking hell!

DENISE. It's okay.

ANNA. What kind of a person *am* I?

DENISE. You're a good person, Anna. (*Beat.*) You're a good person.

Long pause.

ANNA. I'd love to have seen you together.

DENISE. Why?

ANNA. Seen what you were like.

DENISE. We weren't as demonstrative.

ANNA. As him and me?

DENISE. Yeah.

ANNA. Good.

DENISE. But he...

ANNA. Good. I fucking hope you weren't.

DENISE. Ah, no. But he showed his, often, his love in other ways, I suppose.

ANNA. What kind of ways?

DENISE. Agh...

ANNA (*pause*). Don't be shy.

DENISE. Well, you know what he used to do? It's stupid, but, you know crosswords?

ANNA. Uh-huh.

DENISE. I mean, maybe he did this with you as well. He used to make these kind of crosswords, like, draw them and give them to me to solve. And the clues, or the answers, I mean, to the clues, were always, like, things we'd done together.

ANNA (*beat*). Okay.

DENISE. Romantic things. Did he ever do that with you?

ANNA. No.

DENISE. Right. No, like, for example, there was one, what was it… ? (*Beat*.) 'Church of Chips.' One clue, like, and that was in reference to a time we bought chips in Leo Burdock's and brought them over to Christchurch and had them outside…

ANNA. In the grounds, like.

DENISE. Yeah.

ANNA. And was that the answer?

DENISE. 'Christchurch'?

ANNA. Yeah.

DENISE. It was, but the reason it was so memorable was that there was this fellow, we were just having our chips and chatting away or whatever, and this German guy, a tourist, came over, at least I think he was German, and said, 'It is very pleasant to see two people who are so obviously in love.'

ANNA. Really?

DENISE. Yeah.

ANNA. That's so lovely.

DENISE. Isn't it? (*Beat*.) And off he went and that's when Oliver said, you know, for the very first time, 'I *am* in love.' Declared it, like.

ANNA. And did you declare it back?

DENISE. Of course.

ANNA. That's beautiful, Denise.

DENISE. Mm. (*Beat*.) But, anyway, that was the kind of thing he'd put in the…

ANNA. Right.

DENISE. …you know…

ANNA....the crossword.

DENISE. Yeah.

Long pause.

So, when are you gonna come and meet your nephew?

ANNA. God, well, when would you like me to?

DENISE. I dunno, Saturday, say?

ANNA. This Saturday?

DENISE. Yeah, I could make us lunch or...

ANNA. Okay...

DENISE. Yeah?

ANNA....Great. No, Saturday lunch sounds perfect.

DENISE. Excellent. Oh, you'll love him!

ANNA. No, sure I'm sure I will.

Long pause.

What?

DENISE. I want you to know that nothing like that's ever going to happen again, Anna.

ANNA. Nothing like what?

DENISE. Like Oliver. I dunno. Like anything that'll ever cause any kind of rift, or...

ANNA. Oh, me neither.

DENISE....or anger between us.

ANNA. Me neither, Denise.

DENISE. And we'll always talk about things, won't we? Talk them out.

ANNA. We will.

DENISE. Any issues...

ANNA. Yes.

DENISE.…or problems.

ANNA. Of course we will.

DENISE. I'm so fucking sorry, Anna.

ANNA. Stop.

DENISE. I am.

ANNA. Me too, Denise. I know, it's like, 'What a waste of
fucking time…!'

DENISE. It is.

ANNA. I mean, isn't it?

DENISE. Yes.

ANNA. '…and energy.'

DENISE. What a *stupid* waste of time and energy.

ANNA. Stupid. Exactly.

Long pause.

DENISE. Do you know what I was thinking, actually?

ANNA. What?

DENISE. If Mam and Dad had've been alive, I bet what
happened between us never would've happened. Well, it
might have, but…

ANNA. No, but I know what you mean. It never would've
gone *on*.

DENISE. It couldn't have.

ANNA. No.

DENISE. They would've forced us to reconcile.

ANNA. Guilt-tripped us into it.

DENISE. Mm.

ANNA. I mean, wouldn't they?

DENISE. Oh, I've no fucking *doubt* they would've, Anna.

Pause.

ANNA. Do you think about them often?

DENISE. Yeah.

ANNA. Me too. There are days I really feel their absence badly, actually.

DENISE. Really?

ANNA. Mm.

DENISE. Like, how?

ANNA. Well, bad enough I'd be crying.

DENISE. Right. Even after all this time.

ANNA. I just… (*Beat.*) I always felt, when they were alive, even when I didn't see them for periods of time, that they were kind of like a rock.

DENISE. A rock?

ANNA. Not a rock. Like, a sanctuary…

DENISE. I felt that.

ANNA. …you know? Did you feel that? Their very existence in the world was like… (*Beat.*) I don't know…

DENISE. A beacon, is it?

ANNA. Yeah. Or a place of warmth out there in the fucking void, which…

DENISE (*beat*). What?

ANNA. Nothing… which isn't there any more, because, since they went, and more so lately, actually, it just feels that bit colder, I suppose. And darker, and… (*Beat; then, becoming emotional.*) Not literally, obviously…

DENISE. Oh, Anna.

ANNA. …Metaphorically.

DENISE. Anna. Hey.

ANNA. I'm sorry.

DENISE (*also becoming emotional*). That's okay. That's okay.

ANNA (*beat*). Shit.

DENISE. That's okay.

   Silence.

   You okay?

ANNA. Yeah.

DENISE. All right. You sure?

ANNA. Are you?

DENISE. Yeah, I'm fine. Pair of fucking idiots! (*Pause.*) You know what? Let's make a promise to one another here and now… You listening?

ANNA. Yeah.

DENISE. Let's promise each other to be each *other's* beacon, will we? Or to try to be at least. And it'll give us comfort knowing we're there, each of us, is there for the other, like Mam and Dad were always there for us, whenever one of us *needs* the other, yeah?

ANNA. Yeah.

DENISE. Cool.

   Long pause.

   Anyway… I'm gonna have to go in a minute.

ANNA. Oh, really?

DENISE. Yeah.

ANNA. Okay. That's a shame.

DENISE. But, listen: what a lovely chat!

ANNA. Absolutely. Oh, no, I loved it, Denise!

DENISE. Laughter…

ANNA. Yep.

DENISE.…tears…

ANNA. Tears. Indeed.

DENISE. And so, Saturday, yeah?

ANNA. Hm? Oh, for lunch!

DENISE. Yeah.

ANNA. Absolutely.

DENISE. What time?

ANNA. Well, one, I'd assume, 'd be…

DENISE. Yeah, no, one is perfect. (*As they both stand up*.) Sure I'll talk to you before then in any case. Oh, Conor's gonna be mad about you!

ANNA. I hope so.

DENISE. You 'hope so'! Of course he is. (*Beat*.) I love you, sis.

ANNA. Love *you*.

They embrace.

See you.

DENISE. Bye.

She exits.

ANNA *sits back down.*

Entering:

CORA. Sorry about that.

ANNA. That's okay.

CORA (*sitting down*). So, yeah… What were we talking about?

ANNA. Em…

CORA. Shit.

ANNA.…your book.

CORA. That's right. Well, the book was the only reason I came into town in the first place.

ANNA. Right.

CORA. So, they didn't have it in Eason's…

ANNA. Okay.

CORA.…so I went down to Chapters and they didn't have it either, which is *very* surprising, actually, given, you know, the fact that it's so well known, or whatever…

ANNA. Right.

CORA.…or, you know…

ANNA. Like, a classic.

CORA. Exactly. So, anyway. It wasn't there, so I had to turn around and come all the way back, then, across the river, all the way over to Dawson Street.

ANNA. To Hodges Figgis.

CORA. Yeah.

ANNA. And is that where you got it?

CORA. It is, thank God. Finally!

ANNA. Right.

CORA. Although, you know what? If it had've been in one of the other shops, I wouldn't have bumped into *you*…

ANNA. That's true.

CORA.…and I'm delighted I did, so…

ANNA. Listen: me too… so it all worked out in the end.

CORA. Exactly.

ANNA (*beat*). And, what was the panic, anyway?

CORA. What do you mean? To get it?

ANNA. Yeah.

CORA. Well, there wasn't a *panic*. Just it's supposed to be a fairly difficult read…

ANNA. Oh, right. You mean long? Or…

CORA. No, more just in the way that it's written, I think. I dunno. Again, this is only what I've been told.

ANNA. And how much time do you *have*?

CORA. Two weeks?

ANNA. Okay.

CORA. Yeah, I know. I mean, we decided on it a month-and-a-half ago, but, typically, I'm only getting around to buying the thing at the last bloody minute.

ANNA. No, sure that'd be me as well. (*Beat.*) And do you enjoy all that?

CORA. All what? The club, like?

ANNA. Yeah.

CORA. Ah, I do, yeah. (*Beat.*) I mean, I'm not always sure what people are talking about, to be honest? Or, I am, but a lot of the time, I'm thinking, 'Jesus, that's not what *I* got from it at all.'

ANNA. Really?

CORA. Yeah.

ANNA. And would you say that?

CORA. No. *God*, no.

ANNA. Why not?

CORA. I just wouldn't have the confidence, really.

ANNA. Right.

CORA. There's a few there, now, are really smart, you know? Like, *really* smart, so I tend to keep a fairly low profile.

ANNA. You're smart.

CORA. Yeah, well, not as smart as some of them, I can tell you. (*Beat.*) But I do enjoy it. (*Beat.*) I do. And, of course, it gives me something to do at night besides, I dunno, watch TV or whatever.

ANNA. Why, would you not be out much otherwise?

CORA. No, not really.

ANNA. Why not?

CORA. I just wouldn't.

ANNA. So, there isn't a man in your life.

CORA. No, unfortunately. There was for a while there, actually, but...

ANNA (*on 'but'*). Was there?

CORA. Yeah.

ANNA. And what was his name?

CORA. Noah?

ANNA. Right.

CORA. ...but...

ANNA. Like with the Ark.

CORA. Exactly.

ANNA. And how did *that* end? (*Beat.*) Like, did *he* leave *you*? Or...

CORA. No, I left him.

ANNA. Why?

CORA. Ah... (*Beat.*) he wasn't the nicest guy.

ANNA. Ah, no.

CORA. Mm.

ANNA. In what way?

CORA. He just wasn't. You don't wanna hear about it, Anna.

ANNA. Of course I do. This is terrible!

CORA. Well, it's over, which is…

ANNA. Right. Well, which is the crucial thing.

CORA. Exactly.

ANNA. Go on, though. How was he not the nicest guy?

CORA. He was a bully.

ANNA. Really?! What would he do?

CORA. Different things.

ANNA. Like what?

CORA. Like undermine me…

ANNA. Right.

CORA.…or find fault with things I did. Pretty much all the time, like…

ANNA. No.

CORA.…or, yeah, or accuse me of being with other men, even though it was physically impossible since I more or less spent every spare minute I had with him.

ANNA. That's awful, Cora…

CORA. I know.

ANNA.…My God.

CORA. But *I* was a fool, of course, for allowing it to go on as long as it did. I mean…

ANNA. How long was it?

CORA. Well, we went out for about a year, but this went on for seven, eight months of that?

ANNA. Well…

CORA. I know.

ANNA. Well, no, I mean, Jesus, we all know how hard it is to break up with someone we're mad about, *however* fucked up the relationship is.

CORA. I suppose.

ANNA. And what else would he do?

CORA. What else?

ANNA. Uh-huh.

CORA (*beat*). He hit me a couple of times...

ANNA. He did not! Like, slapped you?

CORA. Slapped me, punched me...

ANNA. He didn't punch you!

CORA (*showing inside her mouth*). See that?

ANNA. Oh, Cora...!

CORA. He did that.

ANNA.... You poor thing! And are you okay *now*? I mean, are you over it?

CORA. Ah, yeah.

ANNA. Are you sure?

CORA. No, I am.

ANNA. I'm fucking astonished, Cora!

CORA. Mm.

    Pause.

    You know what's been slightly harder, though, to get over? It's weird.

ANNA. What?

CORA. Him.

ANNA. Okay.

CORA. You know what I mean? I mean, even after the things he did, or how he behaved...

ANNA. …you miss him.

CORA. Yeah.

ANNA. Sure that's understandable.

CORA. Is it?

ANNA. Of course, sure why wouldn't you if you loved him?

CORA. True.

ANNA. …you know?

CORA. And I did. (*Beat.*) I do.

ANNA. You do?!

CORA. Well, that's what I'm saying…

ANNA. You can never go back to him, though.

CORA. No, no. Sure…

ANNA. Cora…

CORA. Sure I wouldn't, Anna, Jesus.

ANNA. Ever.

CORA. Not in a million years, are you joking?! All I'm saying is, it's annoying how, you know, even though someone has hurt you and is bad for you…

ANNA. *Dangerous* to you.

CORA. Absolutely… that doesn't necessarily lessen…

ANNA. Right.

CORA. …or, whatever, dilute the feelings you have for them.

ANNA. True.

CORA. …That's all.

ANNA. No, that *is* annoying, all right.

Pause.

Fucking love, huh?

CORA. Mm.

Long pause.

I love your bracelet, actually.

ANNA. This?

CORA. Yeah, can I have a look?

ANNA. Of course. (*Taking it off and giving it to her.*) I only got it, like, a week or two ago.

CORA. How much was it?

ANNA. Eighty-nine euro?

CORA. That's not bad.

ANNA. Sure it's not? I actually saw one on a woman in Marks and Spencer's and had to go over and ask where she got it.

CORA. And where did she get it?

ANNA. Weirs. You know on Grafton Street?

CORA. Uh-huh.

ANNA. So I went in, whenever, the following weekend and got myself one. You know who I met on the way there, actually?

CORA. Who? (*Handing it back.*) It's gorgeous, Anna.

ANNA. Thanks. Remember Emily Dowling?

CORA. Yeah.

ANNA. Her mother.

CORA. Oh, really. How was she?

ANNA. She was okay. Very haggard looking, actually.

CORA. Right. Well, she would be, though, wouldn't she.

ANNA. No, but remember how stunning she was back then?

CORA. And did you speak to her?

ANNA. Yeah...

CORA. I *do* remember.

ANNA....just for a minute or two. She was asking how I was getting on in life. Was I married...

CORA. Right.

ANNA....had I kids, whatever...

CORA. And did she talk about Emily?

ANNA. Yeah, a bit.

CORA. What was she saying?

ANNA. Just that she misses her still.

CORA. Uh-huh. And what else?

ANNA. Nothing else. Just weird to have met her, you know?

CORA. Mm.

Pause.

Emily. Jesus.

ANNA. Yeah, I know. Remember the sandals?

CORA. God. No, what *I* re...

ANNA. Horrible.

CORA. Absolutely.

ANNA. Sorry.

CORA. No, just saying, that time she ran away...

ANNA. Oh, *that* was fucked. Up the mountain?

CORA. Yeah.

ANNA. That was *weird*, now.

CORA. You know what was weird? No, it was, all right, but you know what was *freaky*?

ANNA. What?

CORA....Or *I* thought it was. The fact that she stayed up there so fucking *long*...

ANNA. No, I know.

CORA.... without any heat or whatever, shelter. I mean,
    I wouldn't have lasted one night, let alone three.

ANNA. I wouldn't have gone up there in the first place.

CORA. Mm.

    Beat.

ANNA. She had a fire, though, didn't she?

CORA. Did she? Oh, that's right.

ANNA. Sure that's how they spotted her.

CORA (*on 'her'*). That's right. But still, though, you know?

ANNA. Oh, no, definitely. (*Beat.*) Hard to comprehend.

CORA. Her doing it?

ANNA. Hm?

CORA. Her running away?

ANNA. Any of it. The running away...

CORA. Well...

ANNE.... the suicide...

CORA. No, I know, but the problem was, though, I mean,
    I remember in school...

ANNA. Well, she wouldn't talk to you.

CORA. Right.

ANNA. I mean, ever. That's right. I mean, there were several
    times before *and* after she ran away I tried to communicate
    with her...

CORA. Yeah, me too.

ANNA. You were *very* good to her, actually, were you not?

CORA. Well, I tried to be, but you know what? If you want my
    help, then give me some *indication* you want it, you know?

I remember once, a free class in the assembly hall, all right? Forty-five minutes I tried to engage with her. And nothing…

ANNA. Right.

CORA. …Blood from a fucking, I dunno…

ANNA. A stone.

CORA. Hm?

ANNA. Blood from a stone.

CORA. Well, it was. I mean, you do your best to be nice to, or to connect to someone, but after a while you just kind of have to admit to yourself, I mean, don't you…?

ANNA. No, you do.

CORA. …that you're wasting your time, you know?

ANNA. Mm.

Long pause.

CORA. It wasn't really that big a surprise, though, was it? Or it was, but in retrospect.

ANNA. That she'd do what she did?

CORA. Uh-huh.

ANNA. In the end, like? No, it wasn't, really.

CORA (*beat*). Because, I mean, how fucked-up a place would you have to be in your head, like…

ANNA. No, I know.

CORA. …to spend three nights in the… And it was winter too. It was cold. The *nights* were cold, I mean, can you imagine? (*Beat.*) Up there on your own…

ANNA. Mm-hm.

CORA. …in the dark. Jesus…

ANNA. I know.

CORA (*beat*)....with only your little fire to keep you warm.

Silence.

Black.

A Nick Hern Book

The Approach first published in Great Britain in 2018 as a paperback original by Nick Hern Books Limited, The Glasshouse, 49a Goldhawk Road, London W12 8QP in association with Landmark Productions

The Approach copyright © 2018 Mark O'Rowe

Mark O'Rowe has asserted his moral right to be identified as the author of this work

Front cover: photography by Patrick Redmond; graphic design by Gareth Jones

Designed and typeset by Nick Hern Books, London
Printed in Great Britain by Mimeo Ltd, Huntingdon, Cambridgeshire PE29 6XX

A CIP catalogue record for this book is available from the British Library

ISBN 978 1 84842 743 3